Little

Victories

Conquering
Unemployment

Tom Brophy

memsender press

memsender press

860 Lower Ferry Road Suite 1
West Trenton, NJ 08628
email: marketing@memsender.com

memsender press is the book publishing division of memsender, inc., an electronic publishing company that provides electronic publishing tools to web sites, and packages intellectual content including books, sounds, games and images for electronic licensing.

ISBN Number: 978-1-452-85461-8

Praise for *Little Victories* and Tom Brophy

During the first few weeks of my unemployment in 2009, I had the good fortune to be introduced to **Little Victories** by Tom Brophy who asked me to provide input to his draft. I eagerly accepted. Little did I realize how helpful and therapeutic this "editorial" endeavor would become in my summer of transition.

For me, the introduction to **Little Victories** could not have been more timely to help me process my feelings and to offer practical direction. **Little Victories** helped ease my stress by teaching me that what I was experiencing was perfectly natural and expected.

Little Victories includes many helpful tools to guide you through the stages of unemployment from dealing with the emotional challenges to preparing to conduct your job search. When you need them the most, **Little Victories** reinforces the importance of small victories – in support of your psyche, your job search, and those around you.

> David Ellison
> VP, Compensation & Benefits

As an HR executive, I have been too often on the other side of the process, and have seen the debilitating effect it takes on an individual who gets the news that they no longer are employed. I recommend *Little Victories* as a must read for anyone who has been terminated for any reason.

Little Victories gives a complete and concise overview of the emotional process that one experiences along with recommended actions to take in getting back into the job market.

J. "Tony" Boccanfuso

Little Victories offers a compelling and informative approach to surviving the hardships of a job loss, and overcoming them to land a new job. Tom's experience and passion are clear in every page of his advice.

Tony Lee, Publisher
CareerCast.com

After many attempts and countless prayer, I can proudly say that I am happily employed. And Mr. Brophy was the first person I called.

Thank you Tom! Again!

Mimi Hamilton

About the Author

Unemployment industry veteran **Tom Brophy** has helped thousands of professionals negotiate the emotional and financial trauma of unemployment.

Little Victories will guide you in dealing with the rejection and depression that comes with unemployment.

Brophy identifies the three major sources of rejection, and shares techniques to get you back in the workplace. Your guideposts through the maze and uneasiness of unemployment, Brophy's proven principles create **"victories"** that lead directly to feeling better about yourself and improving your chances of employment.

These principles, distilled from over 40,000 one-on-one interviews with unemployed professionals, have resulted in 92% back-to-work in 5.2 months. (The average unemployed professional, who earned a salary of $60,000 or more per year, is out of work for 13.5 months.) By creating "victories" and avoiding rejection, you can build confidence, reclaim your self-esteem, and return to being the proud and successful human being that you deserve to be.

Acknowledgements

I would like to thank some of the amazing people who helped me in this twelve year journey – the many good people who encouraged me and without whom this book would not have been written.

Foremost are the many clients who shared their emotions with me, and who taught me through their own experiences the importance of emphasizing life's victories.

Many people in the state unemployment office were instrumental in developing these ideas and enabling me to conduct seminars. Whatever you may have heard about state workers is not true in the NJ unemployment offices: these people are stretched thin (especially today) and are doing their best to help the unemployed.

Thank you Dave McGuire, my former manager who allowed me to do seminars, and Pam Hawley Jones who helped me read computer screens since I had never used a computer prior to working for the state.

Thank you Dan Barus who sat in on my seminars and believed in my message, David Socolow, former Commissioner of Labor who encouraged me to keep going, and Henry Macadam, dear friend and advisor, who helped edit and proofread the text.

Thank you Tony Lee, *Wall Street Journal* editor, who published my articles in "Employment Weekly" and careerjournal.com, and Dave Ellison, dear friend and HR person who told me I was on to something.

Special thanks to my friend and most significant other, Jeri Munday, who encouraged me and spent many nights alone while I wrote this.

Finally, thank you Jon Bartels, a constant supporter and good friend, and Glenn Paul, my publisher with whom I magically reconnected after 30 years.

While I often felt like the Lone Ranger, an army of friends and associates have kept alive my belief in this message and this mission. Thank you all.

    Tom Brophy

Table of Contents

A Light at the End of the Tunnel? "Y.A." and Me: How I Met a Giant "Momentum" – Turning Defeats into Victories – Getting Results – Some Rules for the Road

"I Haven't Got a Clue" Odd Person Out Syndrome – Stay Cool – Keep Your Anger Out of Interviews – Customizing Strategy – One Size DOESN'T Fit All – Establishing Your Plan for Victory – How Disappointment Improved John Bidwell's Life

Introduction

I spent 18 years with the New Jersey Department of Labor in the unemployment division. I certainly never thought I'd wind up there, but career paths don't always turn out the way we expect.

In 18 years, I spoke one-on-one with thousands of unemployed people. In most cases, we met for an eligibility interview where I verified their claims and made sure they were doing everything necessary to remain eligible for their benefits. I was eager to succeed, and, like most rookies, I followed the procedure to the letter. I had my interview form and simply went down the list looking for job prospects, phone calls, contacts made, etc.

As time passed, I discovered I had a lot in common with the group I'll call "first timers." You see, I was unemployed before joining the state workforce, having owned my own business, a shoe store, for more than 20 years. When it closed, I was lost and devastated – and I had no idea how to get through each day, much less find a job. With no energy or self esteem, I felt unwanted and scared to death. How ironic it was to land a job through networking with friends. I spent each day hearing the same pain I'd felt myself only months before.

As I grew more comfortable in my role as an interviewer, I'd occasionally ask, "How are you feeling?" or "How do you spend your time?" Once candidates sensed that I was genuinely interested in them, they often broke down and cried. I had hit a nerve, and it was revealing. They were somewhere they'd never been before, yet they were expected to fall into place and accept their plight.

Because I truly cared, I developed a program called TLC (Transition Layoff Counseling) and would suggest to certain candidates that they attend my weekly TLC seminars. Each week, I spent 90 minutes with 25 to 30 people giving them feedback and instructions based on the one-on-one interviews. Afterward, I tracked their progress. To my amazement, by demonstrating the danger of rejection and the value of victories, 92% were back to work in 5 months.

I went on to become the supervisor of claims examiners and the manager of the local office over the next 15 years, but I never forgot the gut-wrenching feeling of becoming unemployed. I've helped thousands of people by implementing the principles in *Little Victories*, and I hope that this book will help you establish your own victories, a new job and a happier life.

Chapter 1

The Secret Life of the Unemployed

"Come on Joe, snap out of it! Things are going to be fine." Sound familiar? People are always trying to help the unemployed professional, but they only make things worse. Don't they? They seem to think that saying "Snap out of it" will magically produce a wave of calmness and all will be well. Or it will happen when they say, "Keep doing what you're doing; there's a light at the end of the tunnel."

What they don't know is that, to the unemployed professional, the light at the end of the tunnel is a freight train coming head on.

Unemployment is a world unto itself where we are suddenly thrust into a new "neighborhood" and are expected to know exactly what to do. We didn't ask to be here, but here we are because our employer suddenly decided to downsize or eliminate our department and, within hours, our world is turned upside down.

We're numb, and we spend the next three months going through the motions – not grasping what really has happened. We follow orders because we don't dare question anyone or anything. We begin to send out resumes and act like everything is going according to plan. We are lost and confused, but can never tell a soul. The pain inside is so intense that, rather than divulge this, we make an immediate pact with ourselves that we will never tell anyone. We will take this secret to the grave with us.

That about sums up the first three months of being unemployed. You can throw in a hundred non-responses from resumes, a few hundred "no's" on the telephone and an overwhelming feeling of not belonging, and there you have it: we have become someone whom nobody wants and who absolutely doesn't have what anyone is looking for. We are trapped in a world where everyone else is employed, and our isolation gets worse and worse.

We rehash our separation from our job over and over and become certain that there must have been something we could have done to save our job. Our relationships slowly deteriorate and we don't like ourselves very much. Our new neighborhood, "Unemploymentville," is very scary because everyone thinks we're progressing when, in reality, we are rapidly regressing.

The mere fact that we don't belong serves as a constant reminder that we are on the outside looking in, and the outlook is bleak.

How do we begin to make progress without giving our fear away? Why does time become our enemy, and filling our day with productive efforts become an impossible task? Why is our energy level on empty? Is there anyone out there who knows how desperate we have become? Why do we constantly talk to ourselves and get no positive answers?

These questions and many more like them only point out that unemployment has symptoms and all of these feelings and fears are a direct result of these symptoms taking over.

We feel betrayed, abandoned, bewildered and somehow responsible for having lost our job. These symptoms, if left unattended, can potentially destroy us. Yes, DESTROY us. They are all derived from REJECTION and we are allergic to REJECTION. If I give you a constant dose of something to which you're allergic, you will die. This is serious. It is not to be taken lightly and we cannot assume it will suddenly stop and the job will materialize.

It is a process that requires an understanding of our new circumstances and a game plan to affect a positive change. I have a game plan that has worked time and again. The plan focuses on establishing victories and avoiding rejection. Think of a field filled with land mines. Your job is to cross the field and avoid the land mines. The land mines are rejection and are there at every step.

You've been following orders, religiously sending out resumes and making boring phone calls. But, unknown to you, those resumes ARE the enemy. They are the source of rejection, disguised as your ally. They are the largest source of rejection on planet earth.

The average unemployed professional sends out 116 resumes in the first three months and gets six responses. That means a total of 110 rejections, which translates into a lot of pain. What unemployed professionals don't know is that 92% of resumes are NEVER read. So why would you do something that constantly causes pain? The answer is simple: we are gullible and we are vulnerable. These two characteristics cause a great deal of trouble. We assume we are doing the right thing because we are following universally accepted directions.

Let's put it another way. Ever been in a strange town and asked for directions? How do you know the directions are right? You don't. You assume they are and innocently do as you are told. Rarely do we wonder if the directions might be wrong. We are gullible about an employment system that does not operate as advertised, and that eventually causes rejection and depression.

Imagine the family "breadwinners" as machines requiring 10 gallons of gas each day to function and run smoothly. When life is normal, breadwinners gets five gallons (victories or ego builders) from their jobs and five gallons from their families. Now, the job is suddenly eliminated, and the breadwinner is five victories short every day. Without the required number of gallons or victories each day, the machine slows down, and then stops.

Unfortunately, the family sees their breadwinner at the onset of unemployment as the same person. The family is completely unaware that the breadwinner is running on empty. Children and spouses go about their lives in the same way, providing the five victories daily, but unable to see the internal devastation and damage. Only after three months go by do they begin to see our pain, and, at that point, it is too late.

The unemployed professional has been grasping for victories or fuel for three months, and, in a twisted state of mind, takes the blame for being a failure. He or she looks in the mirror each night and says, "How can someone fall so far, so fast?" Meanwhile, other family members can't see the internal strife that has been taking place. They can't see guilt or resentment or anger or fear. They can't see or hear the daily conversations that the unemployed professional is having with their "inner self". What they see is a parent or spouse who appears to be a little irritable at times while they search for a job. Oh, if only they knew!

I'm sure for many of you I've already mentioned a feeling or a situation that has struck a nerve. That's OK. I'm glad I did because if I hadn't you would have put this book down after the first page. Something else you need to know is that these symptoms do not manifest themselves in the first week or the third week or even the seventh week. **It isn't until somewhere between week eight and week twelve that they begin to surface and become a burden.**

The first month we are totally numb and simply groping our way along. We try our hardest to look and sound "normal" while protecting our fragile vulnerability. Somewhere between week 10 and 13, we come to the realization that we really have no clue what we're doing; then, keeping it a secret becomes one of our primary responsibilities. Our tone of voice must always be upbeat and we must always carefully choose our words and say the right thing.

We need to brag about our resumes and how many we're sending out each week. We need to sell everyone on the idea that we are on schedule. Naturally, all of this is on the outside and is nothing more than a Hollywood screenplay or a TV script. We present ourselves as someone who has everything under control. All the while, we are slowly and painfully dying on the inside. Our ability to reason is slowly leaving us. Suddenly, knowing who to call and what to say when we get them on the phone becomes a chore. For this and for the other feelings, there is a logical explanation.

You see, we all have an imaginary, old-fashioned "balance scale" within our brain. When things are normal, the two "pans" of the scale are evenly balanced and we are able to function. Six months ago, we were thinking clearly and making daily, mature decisions. Here we are six months down the road, and we seem light years away from thinking clearly. We have become paralyzed and unable to make the simplest of decisions.

Why? Because one side of the scale has been weighted down with rejection, making it impossible to think or feel normally. Or, put another way, we have given ourselves daily doses of poison in the form of rejection and have slowly wasted away. What is the cure? How do we recover? What do we do?

We need to get that scale back to normal balance as fast as we can. We need to eliminate the rejection immediately. We need to stop poisoning ourselves. <u>We need to learn how to create victories and not defeats.</u> Victories give us the energy and drive to make things happen. We don't realize how important they are to our daily life. Some examples of victories and encouragements are 1) a great mark on a test 2) being asked to dance at a party 3) owning our first car 4) being accepted at college 5) graduating from college 6) getting that first job 7) getting a raise 8) getting married 9) buying a house, and, generally, progressing through our lives.

We have many daily victories that go unheralded such as the ability to pay a mortgage or buy a car or pay tuition. These necessities are sometimes overlooked as important victories. Every day of our lives is filled with events that are either rejections or victories. The people who succeed and appear positive and upbeat are the ones who have more victories than rejection. It is that simple.

Here is an example of a "victory" in the world of unemployment: six months ago, a returned phone call was an everyday occurrence and now it is a major victory. That returned phone call says that someone has recognized you and acknowledged your existence. What makes it more important is that we get a lot of mileage out of a small victory. It shows just how important small victories are to our physical and mental make-up. We can get by for a day or two with a little victory.

Losing our job devastates more than our paycheck and our health benefits. We lose communication skills, relationships, sleep and appetite. We have such a hunger to be back in the "loop" because, as human beings, we need to belong. If we could whisper a message into the ear of our former employer without fear of any embarrassment, it would sound something like this. "Mr. Employer, you have no idea what you did to me when you took away my right to earn a living."

Not being able to provide for ourselves and our loved ones is a tremendous blow to our egos because it means we have to rely on some sort of public assistance in order to survive. The immediate job loss stuns us, but the responsibility of figuring out what to do next is the knockout punch.

The symptoms of unemployment also possess a particular characteristic: embarrassment. We don't like to talk about the internal devastation so it's very difficult to detect by our family and close friends. When we have a serious health problem, we go to the hospital and are asked, "Where does it hurt?" We then point to a particular part of our body and, within a few minutes, the treatment begins.

In unemployment, there is no single place to point to because the pain is everywhere AND we don't want to talk about it. We have become a patient who looks the same, lives in the same house and drives the same car, but is secretly dying inside and – oh, yes – doesn't want to talk about it. So we continue to ingest daily doses of rejection, continue to force a smile, and continue to experience the most private pain on earth. That is a real dilemma for our loved ones and a disaster for us.

Does that strike a nerve? I hope so. I needed to because you need to be around people who speak your own language. You need to "let it go" and trust again. Depending on how long you have been out of work, I can tell you exactly what symptoms you're exhibiting and pinpoint where you are.

For example, after about eight weeks you begin to feel the effects of ending up in places like Trader Joes and Wal-Mart on a Tuesday morning at 10:00 a.m., and you have the distinct feeling people around you can sense you don't belong there. You feel very conspicuous because at 10:00 a.m. on a weekday, you're normally working. Aren't you? You can feel the stares and all eyes are on you.

You're not the only one in that situation. Other unemployed professionals may be in the store with you, so we begin to have rapid conversations with ourselves and, before very long, we've left the store. We don't want to be in that store any more, do we? That begins the transition to staying home and not being seen anywhere that brings attention to us. How am I doing so far, readers? Can you see yourself in this situation?

OK, you have now identified the various symptoms that you have experienced and are probably feeling rather helpless about. Well, you can be absolutely certain that you are not alone and that everyone who has read this book up to this point feels exactly the same way. There is no exception, there is no variation, and there is no deviation.

Your next and very important job is to be aware of, and to avoid, the "invisible traffic jam". We all dislike traffic jams, but, being an unemployed professional, you are in the largest traffic jam on earth. In the first three months of unemployment (approximately 100 days), you send out 116 resumes and get six responses. That means a total of 100 rejections, correct? Why?

How many resumes do you think are generated if an ad is posted for a sales manager at $100,000 per year in job-posting medium such as *The New York Times*, *Wall Street Journal*, Monster.com, or Career Builder.com? About 800 per day or 4000 per week. **SO HOW DOES ANY EMPLOYER FIND YOU?** It's impossible – or, at least, extremely random. The problem is that we can't see the traffic jam. Everyone is doing the exact same thing.

This is not your fault. We become more and more depressed because no one has responded to our resume. We are not aware that 92% of resumes are **NEVER** read. For three months we have been doing what we're told to do or what we perceive to be the right approach, and all we get back is pain. You need to be able to see the enemy. When the enemy is invisible, there is a serious problem.

Imagine driving a car on any stretch of highway and suddenly cars are backed up for half a mile. I suddenly hop out of a traffic helicopter, run up to your car, stick a microphone in your window and ask "Why aren't you moving?" Your response is rather a sarcastic retort. Now imagine this: what if all the cars in front of you and all the cars behind you are suddenly invisible? What would you say then? You are not moving and you have no idea why.

That is where you are. The problem is invisible. You can't see the thousands of resumes submitted along with yours, and all the resumes that end up in the circular file. You've assumed your resume was read and that you were eliminated as a candidate for the job. You have had that sickening feeling that your credentials were just not good enough. When that happens 100 times within 100 days, you've reached a critical stage of rejection. You've ingested too much poison and are deteriorating rapidly. You are in dire need of the only cure: an immediate victory followed by plenty of others. You need to start gaining some positive momentum and to begin accumulating victories. Allow yourself to have something good happen.

You have made important decisions in your life. Now that you understand your position as a family breadwinner – maybe THE family breadwinner – it is time to make this firm commitment to yourself: stop doing whatever you have been doing. <u>Starting today, you are going to change your plan and do nothing but win.</u> You are going to become very selective as to how you spend your time. You are going to take care of yourself and not allow yourself to get anywhere near a rejection. You are a winner, and it's time to show it.

What I have provided the unemployed professionals in the last twelve years is a gentle push in the right direction. I'm able to give them a little opening in that blank wall of rejection through which they can see that there is blue sky ahead. They sense very quickly that I do know how they feel, and, the moment that happens, everything changes. They begin to open up to allow themselves the luxury of getting in touch with their feelings again. They may even laugh or cry, but at least they are aware that they are feeling again.

Here is something to think about. Those of you who are reading this book and are unemployed already know that average people who have decent jobs, and think their jobs are secure have no idea – none whatsoever – how close they are to total devastation. It only takes four words: "I'm letting you go" or "I'm laying you off." Within 24 hours, life as they knew it is never the same.

Suddenly, "not belonging," being "out of the loop" throws us in a downward spiral that paralyzes us and leaves us afflicted with a feeling we've never felt before. This explains the intense and the deeply emotional responses I get from unemployed professionals. They know I'm not just reciting statistics from books or case files.

I know that what I've learned is 100% accurate and has never once let me down. I know that the people I've spoken with are grateful not only for sharing with them what I've learned from others, but also for the opportunity to share with me their fears and anxieties. They learn quickly that I'm *sympathetic* to their situation and *empathetic* because I've gone through the same experience, which I'll get to shortly.

Similarly, when someone who is grappling with unemployment tells me "thank you" at the end of a conversation, it comes from deep inside. I can't count the number of times that, after taking an extra 10 or 15 minutes during a claims hearing with someone who is hurting from the pain of unemployment, they say, "I can't believe I'm telling all this to someone I've never met before. Most of what I've just told you I haven't shared with my spouse."

In a nutshell, they know that **I know**, and that understanding is the key to the effectiveness of this program. The primary reason for doing what I do is that helping other people is the greatest feeling on earth. I absolutely love what I do. Every day that I connect with someone in need is a victory for me, too. If I can help you, please write to me at **tom@tbrophy.com**

Let me share a little of my journey over the last twenty years that brought me to my present position.

My family founded a men's shoe store in Princeton, New Jersey that operated for nearly a century. It was Princeton's oldest business that was continuously run by the same family.

On New Year's Eve 1980, a man walked into the store with an irritating smirk on his face. That expression is still very vivid and I can remember exactly what he said. "I'm looking for Tom Brophy." I said to him, "I'm Tom Brophy. What can I do for you?" Still smirking, he looked at me, handed me an envelope and said: "Here. This is for you." I opened it and read it. It was my eviction notice.

I was stunned and instantly numb. This notice was given to me by "The Collins Group," the new owners of Palmer Square (35 retail stores in the center of Princeton) who just one month earlier had told me how important our store was and how they were counting on me to be a young leader of this retail community. It is still so vivid and painful that I can remember exactly where I was standing at the time. I had been lied to, betrayed, abandoned and now discarded.

I was a mess. I couldn't sleep, couldn't eat and wasn't able to focus or function. Over the next few years I opened a gift shop in the Princeton Hyatt Hotel and also bought a smoke shop. I tried to move Brophy's Shoe Store a few blocks away but soon learned I was spinning my wheels.

After three years of constant struggle and not making any money, I decided to get out of the retail business. I sold everything at a loss and looked for a new career in the commercial real estate business. I went from the frying pan into the fire. After being evicted and losing my family business, I went on to deal with constant rejection in real estate. That was a major mistake. I was depressed beyond belief and thought I was going to die. There seemed to be nothing I could do and I was surely doomed.

Out of utter desperation, and keeping my word to a friend, I reluctantly kept an appointment with the State of New Jersey for a job interview that he had arranged. At the time, I was still in a state of shock and very, very, depressed. The interview was a blur that I can hardly remember today. I couldn't imagine myself working for the State. I had no expectations, especially in my mental condition.

That's where the miracle begins. Four weeks later, I was told I had a job. There were over 12,000 employees in the Department of Labor and several thousand job title categories. What were the odds of finding myself working in the Unemployment Department and talking to unemployed people on a daily basis? Part of my job was to interview each client about the progress of their job search.

After about four months, I began to notice a pattern because I was seeing the same people every four or five weeks. The complaints and frustrations were similar, regardless of age or gender or previous income. I began to take notes and realized I was hearing the same frustrations I had personally felt months before. Thirteen years later, here I am. Everything written here was learned from unemployed professionals like you who told me what works – and what doesn't.

Little Victories does not find a specific job; it is not a cookie-cutter approach. What it will do is empower you to do things your way. You were successful long before you picked up this book, and <u>you will be successful again</u>. What is different is the momentum that this book will help you create by eliminating *rejection* and building *victories*.

Now is the time for change. You have probably been following the same routine every day and have slowly regressed to a point where you have lost your confidence. An unemployed professional is an eternal optimist who looks for a job in the same way every day, and expects different results. My program consists of the very best ideas from successful job-seekers who have run this gauntlet themselves. This book is a compilation of their wisdom.

Look at it this way: up to now, you've sought employment through the traditionally accepted method of resume-and-rejection. If that's not working, take a step forward by reading on and trying a new approach.

I'll provide concrete examples instead of vague theories that will enable you to recapture your former self and begin to make positive decisions. You *are* a winner and are very capable of getting back into the loop once you identify and understand the problems in the deeply flawed system we call "getting a job."

Chapter 2

What Happens to Unemployed Professionals

Unemployment Shouldn't Be a "Growth Industry."

Providing services to the unemployed professional has become a major business. In fact, it has become a growth "industry" at a time when the economy – local, national and international – has undergone a recession. Not surprisingly, the two phenomena are linked; the business of getting people back to work is most in demand when unemployment is on the rise.

Those services are provided by the State and by private, for-profit companies. State services are free to those seeking re-employment, but are limited by the size of annual budgets and the number of personnel who administer them. Private companies are limited only by the amount that benevolent employers or unemployed workers are willing to spend. In either case, there are no guarantees.

The first step in the state system is for the unemployed to register with a claims representative who will validate the individual's case and determine both the amount and the duration of benefits. That process begins with an application online or by telephone, and is generally followed by a face-to-face session at the unemployment office. More often than not, this is the beginning of a bureaucratic treadmill.

No one will argue that electronic filing represents the most convenient method: new technologies eliminate the need for the claimant to visit the state employment office, which means less demand on state personnel. Questions are asked, information is provided, and benefits, one hopes, are forthcoming.

While filing a new claim electronically is convenient for the unemployed and timesaving for state workers, the automated unemployment claims system works subtly against the newly unemployed. The automated system isolates the newcomer and makes him or her feel even more rejected and depressed. For the newly unemployed, automated filing systems set the tone for the task of finding another job. There is no one to talk with and no feedback: you tell the system about yourself, and wait for a response.

For the unemployed professional who may have held administrative positions, exercised authority over a substantial staff, or who managed a company's financial network, the situation can be particularly alienating.

Defining the Unemployed Professional

Unemployed professionals in New Jersey (where I work, and my home state since birth) are those whose maximum weekly benefits total $600, as determined by the Unemployment Insurance rate set by the Department of Labor. However, as persons, unemployed professionals are those who, unlike seasonal workers, find themselves in a "new neighborhood," that is, among those who are out of work.

Most professionals have never been here before, and the adjustment is tough. Unemployed professionals are often those who had been rewarded with lasting, high-paying, highly skilled jobs, often with full family medical benefits packages and retirement plans. Suddenly, they're faced with a vacuum: no job, no colleagues, no pay and no benefits. They now realize that there is a limit to the amount of their unemployment compensation: a total sum, paid out over a finite number of weeks.

Understandably, they are confused, frustrated and even frightened. They have just been told (sometimes rather abruptly) that they are no longer needed. They are also *vulnerable* and *gullible*, and in need of assurance that they will be assisted by unemployment professionals who are "user friendly" and sensitive to their needs.

Below are some suggestions about how unemployed professionals can make it through this critical and difficult circumstance, and some practical tools and techniques that will get them back into the workplace sooner and more smoothly. In order to understand this advice and implement the tips, it's helpful to understand the facts that are common for all unemployed professionals. Perhaps it is also reassuring to know that you are not on your own.

Symptoms: The Language and Feelings of Unemployment

Unemployment has its own feelings, its own language and – as those who have experienced it know – its own peculiar ailments. It has visible and invisible symptoms (frustration, fear) as well as corresponding outer manifest-tations (behavior, demeanor) that change as the days and weeks go by.

When professionals become unemployed, it is safe to say that it is one of the most private, personal and painful feelings they will ever experience in their lives. In some ways losing a job, especially one with which you've been identified for years, is like losing a part of yourself.

One reason that's true is that unemployment can hit with the suddenness of a car accident. Who hasn't heard of some professional employee who received a "pink slip" on a Wednesday with a request that his or her desk be cleared by Friday? Within the course of a few hours or days, your entire world is upside down.

You are rendered paralyzed and incapable of making simple, everyday decisions. And, like an illness or a disease, what happens to you has an effect far beyond yourself. It impacts your family, friends, neighbors and even your attitude toward complete strangers. Its effects are emotional as well as physical.

Beyond the initial shock to you and to those closest to you, there are certain "markers" or transition points of which you should be aware. There is a noticeable change in the behavior of the unemployed professional between weeks 12 and 16. This change may not be noticed by the individual, but it is obvious to professionals and, often, to your family and friends.

It becomes evident to the observant that you've come from a time of high energy and high hopes (the first three or four months of unemployment) and are now feeling a sense of deep despair and hopelessness. You've been weighed down and ultimately overwhelmed by continual experiences of *rejection*. You feel lost.

The realization that you're no longer "in the club" has finally sunk in, and it is increasingly difficult to regain the feeling that you'll ever be accepted again. You also have a secret that, so far, you've been able to keep from your own family and from your closest friends: while they think you know exactly what to do to regain a job, in reality *you don't have a clue*.

Day after day, you're literally "going through the motions" of job searches and occasional interviews, hoping and praying that this will seem reassuring to those closest to you. But it suddenly strikes you that this is not working, and that the process has become an endless, energy-sapping treadmill.

Even so, you continue to give the impression that all is well, and that employment is just a matter of a "few more days" or "one more interview." It becomes more and more difficult to continue this charade, but you persist with it because so much depends on maintaining optimism in the face of rejection. It is a brave act – but a very lonely one. It can lead to a loss of self-esteem, and to a sense of absolute despair.

This situation develops when three factors coincide: ignorance of the employment system, vulnerability, and gullibility. Not knowing what to do and how to do it (ignorance) is the primary factor in the unemployment nightmare. Getting started "on the wrong foot" is going to lead you inexorably down the path to vulnerability and gullibility, with no return route marked.

Because you don't know even the basic steps of finding employment in a viciously competitive market, you are vulnerable to fatal mistakes in the way you present yourself to prospective employers. Ignorance keeps you unaware of that.

Ignorance fortified by vulnerability will inevitably lead you into situations or decisions in which you will be particularly gullible: that's when an outplacement firm can separate you from what little money you have with no guarantee that you'll have the job in return for their hefty fee.

The most amazing fact is that gender, age and income have nothing to do with these three symptoms. A woman age 33 making $35,000 per year and a man age 60 making $400,000 per year both sound and look very similar by the time they reach week 18 of unemployment. Professional unemployment is an equal opportunity predicament.

The two individuals noted above will sound the same, construct their written sentences the same, will share the same fear and uncertainty, and will spend their days and weekends going through very similar routines. This is a progressive, debilitating problem that must be addressed. In that situation, we are alone and unable to share our secret unless someone with special talents offers to help.

The Three "C's" Approach to Unemployed Professionals

There are three "C's" to keep in mind for the unemployed professional. These are *communication*, *compassion* and *credibility*. All three are equally important and necessary: if *one* is missing, it will completely negate the full effectiveness of the other two. Taken together, these three will produce an "honest relationship" that is the only effective way to improve your perspective and your prospects.

Because of my own personal employment history, I know what it's like to be suddenly out of a job (and I was the owner of the business!) I understand better than most unemployment specialists the psychological problems, but also the psychological *gifts* of unemployment. Unemployed professionals all have a gift that allows them to see right through people who are phony. They are much like a person who suddenly goes blind and, as compensation, his sense of touch increases by six-fold.

Jobless professionals who have lost their privilege to earn a living suddenly find that they must rely on basic forms of communication in order to survive. They need help and practical information so that their new gift – this ability to know when a person is genuine or phony – can provide maximum benefit. Their insight is the most accurate sense on earth and is never wrong.

I can be so sure about this because what I'm writing comes from them, not from me or some unemployment manual created by a committee. I've talked with unemployed professionals for more than a decade: they know what's real and what's not.

The situations and the symptoms that I've touched upon so far are not unique to the State of New Jersey. These conditions exist wherever unemployment exists, and as the economy stagnates and the international situation grows increasingly uncertain, we must, as Ben Franklin said, "all hang together, or most assuredly, we shall all hang separately."

Our country needs you, and our economy needs you as part of the "human capital" that continues to improve the advanced society that we live in. You need to understand how the employment system truly works – or, even more important, does *not* work – so that you can stop talking yourself down, and get back to the everyday victories that bring you happiness, support your family, and contribute to a better world.

Chapter 3

Getting Back to Where You Were

Resumes – How *NOT* To Get Started

What you're told is: get your resume done, fine tune it again and again, make phone calls, set up the interview, and everything will fall into place. Well, it just doesn't work that way, and when someone suddenly unemployed learns that sad fact, it is a shock. It's the beginning of a rejection process that seems endless.

It goes against everything you're told: you learn when young that if you "follow instructions, you'll get to where you want to be." Unfortunately, in the world of unemployment, that just isn't true. The bottom line is that everyone else who's unemployed is on the same "road" and there's a huge and impenetrable "traffic jam" that you can't see. As I mentioned earlier, this is when you become one of 800 resumes a day or 4000 a week. In my TLC seminars, I ask, *"If I'm getting 800 resumes a day, **how do I find you**?"* That's when the light goes on in the heads of those in the seminar room.

The person to whom you send your resume has a small staff. He tells the two or three assistants to go through the 800 resumes on their desks and pick out a few that "look interesting." "Put them aside and throw away the rest." Why do it that way? Because there will be another 800 on their desks tomorrow. And again the next day.

It gets worse when you submit your resume to an online service – which most large companies require. <u>In all likelihood</u>, **no one** <u>ever sees your resume!</u> Computers analyze your resume to match key words for desired traits. You're now grist in a search engine. Some career advisors will tell you to "game" the system by including key phrases from the job posting, so that the computer reading your resume will be more likely to mark you as a likely candidate, which may or may not help because the odds are still stacked high and wide against you.

Here is how computers respond to most resumes. You can fill in the fields:

Dear <your first name>,

Thank you for your interest in <company name>. We have chosen another candidate to fill the <title at company name and company division>. However, your information will be kept on file and considered for future opportunities.

Thanks again for your interest and best of luck to you with your career search.

Regards,
Human Resources

Perhaps you've received these emails. You are not alone. Most applicants don't realize that more than 92% of resumes will go unread by human eyes – or tossed in the trash! No one tells you that in advance because that's a group statistic. The unemployed professional instead learns to deal with the bitter math of personal rejection: "I'm unemployed three months, and in that time, I've sent out 116 resumes. I've received six responses. What does that tell me? It says very clearly that 110 people don't think I'm worth a response. Whatever they're looking for, I don't have it."

Out of 116, six people acknowledge you. Worse yet, the interviews generated by those responses came to nothing. You look in the mirror at night and the conversation consists of one bleak question: "How have I fallen so far, so fast?" This is the reality of the situation, and it is far more common that you might realize. No matter what someone else unemployed might tell you, we all keep tabs of how many resumes we sent out, and how many get a response. "The Math of Despair" is one response for every 20 applications – about a 5% response rate.

Resumes are very frustrating. I rank them about twelfth on the list of important job-finding tools. A resume becomes important AFTER you interview for a job. The resume is a tool to help present the successful candidate to someone else in that company.

What is the best definition of a resume? Most people will say, "It is a composite look at my work history." Sound about right? There are many ways to write a resume but the most important thing is this: a resume must tell in one or two pages how great you are and what great things you've done. What it doesn't tell is far more important to an employer: it doesn't say that you're compassionate or sensitive or neat or that you're a workaholic, a good listener, articulate, trustworthy, nice to be around or even miserable.

It really does not say a whole lot about YOU, so you'll have to get that across in other ways.

Telephone Tales – Making the Phone Your Friend

The next source of rejection is something called the telephone. Telephones used to be our friends, whether we'd used them for family or business. When we become unemployed, telephones become the gate keepers between us and a prospective job. We are dealing with receptionists, assistants, or, worse, voice mail, to make the contacts we need, so it's important to plan these interactions.

Despite the difficulties of making a good phone call, phones are still the best tool we have for making a personal connection. A good phone call like the one I'll tell you about in a moment makes a personal connection and sets up your job interview. That's it! You're looking to literally get your foot in the door.

Please don't try to set up interviews with emails. Don't confuse sending an email with making a connection: you may use email later for supplying follow-up information, but email is too impersonal to make a real, personal connection. It's too easy to block, ignore or say, "No" in an email – and email doesn't convey the warmth and confidence of your voice or enable you to respond to questions. Use your phone to set up your appointments.

Before each call, write a message of approximately 25 seconds. Practice it on a recorder until you sound upbeat and positive. This will prepare you for your short conversation and will also provide an excellent voicemail message. You no longer sound like someone begging for a job (which also sounds boring.) Asking for an interview is not always a comfortable situation, and, if we don't know how to handle it, the call is wasted and the job is lost. I've learned that some unemployed professionals approach a phone conversation "leading with their chin." They're already expecting to be hit, and, very often, that's what happens.

That's one identifiable symptom of unemployment: the loss of confidence has set you up for another failure: "losing" a phone call. As you progress in time through unemployment, those symptoms become more debilitating because you're robbed of energy, and that's easily detectable by others. Prospective employers can sense, see, and hear our loss of enthusiasm. That's NOT what we want to project on the phone, but it's difficult to disguise because it is so rooted in our self-esteem, so we have to over-prepare for our phone conversations. Make sure you're confident and prepared.

Make your time on the phone work FOR you and not AGAINST you. Make the phone your friend!

Here's the most important thing: get through to the person who will decide if you're hired. That's a job in itself. That's the whole game. You have to become a detective. Don't just say, "Please let me speak to the manager." That tells the manager (or head nurse, or department chairperson or whatever is the equivalent title in your profession), "This person on the phone doesn't know who I am." Suddenly, the gate closes and the walls go up. It's like the telemarketing calls we get at home during dinner where the caller says, "I'd like to speak to the man or woman of the house." It's an impersonal approach, and it doesn't work when you're trying to get a job interview.

Know whom you're asking for in advance. Your chances of success are far greater if you know that person's name and what he or she does in that company or institution.

When you do get through, what are you going to say? Most of us may think: "Hi, Mr. Williams. My name in Tom Brophy, and I'd like to talk to you about the ad you ran in the paper." The response is likely to be: "So you've read the ad. What about it?" That's not a good start. There's a better way to use your time on the phone.

Learn how to make an offer. What are you going to do for Steve Williams? What does he need you for? He didn't have you on his staff yesterday, or the day before. You want him to have you on his staff tomorrow, but what can you bring "to the table" that will get Steve Williams' attention? We usually talk too much on the phone, and much of what we say is superfluous.

What I suggest is to get a referral to Mr. Williams. 70% of new jobs are obtained through referrals, and you need a human link to improve the odds of your meeting. This may seem like a daunting task, but it's not. You've probably heard of the idea of "six degrees of separation," which means that, no matter who you are, there is a good chance that you are linked to almost everyone in our society by no more than five or six people.

In the famous Small World Experiment, researchers in Massachusetts sent packages to randomly-selected people in Nebraska and asked them to forward the package to people in the Boston area. If the recipient happened to know the person in Boston, he sent it directly to that person; if not, he might send it to someone in the northeast or perhaps to the Boston area. Eventually, the packages would arrive at their destination, and, to the researchers' surprise, the average number of people in the chain was about six. Would you speak with six people in order to set up a successful job interview?

Here's some good news: in the Internet age, it's even easier to make contacts and get referrals. Internet sites LinkedIn and Facebook are great places to start. LinkedIn is a business network designed to help people make business contacts. Facebook, while a social network, now claims 400 million members. The average person knows about 200 people, so make contact with your friends and ask for their help.

Here are four of the most powerful words ever spoken: "I need your help…." Your friends *want* to help you. <u>Let them help you.</u> Tell them, "I need your help. I need to build a bridge to Mr. Williams at eCloud Systems. Do you know Mr. Williams or anyone at eCloud or anyone in that industry?" If your friends don't know Mr. Williams, they'll know someone who knows him or knows of him, and you'll be one step closer. Work your way through that chain until you can make a call like this:

> Hi, Mr. Williams. I'm Tom Brophy. Our mutual
> friend Jerry Smith asked me to give you a call.
> I have something I want to talk over with you.
> When can we get together?

Short, sweet and to the point. Or, as well-known chef Emeril Lagasse puts it: "Bam!" That approach gets the person's attention and makes them want to find out what it is that you are going to share with them. To use another of Emeril's expressions, you've "Kicked it up a notch!"

That's how you make appointments. *That's* how you use the phone. Allocate about 1½ hours per day to phone calls, which amounts to about 12-14 phone calls during that time period. List the people you're going to call, set aside a specific time to do that, and write down what you're going to say (including how to make that crucial appointment). Don't get off that phone until you've nailed that appointment! What this creates is a personal victory for you. The moment you can make an appointment, you've won a battle with rejection. Someone with a position to offer is willing to listen to you, and your next challenge is to make that person choose <u>you </u>for that job.

One final tip: "google" Mr. Williams before you call him. Everyone worth calling is worth knowing before you call. You may find official biographies, speeches, awards, affiliated charities, and articles that the person has written. You may find common interests that will help you make a personal connection. Ultimately, people do business with people they *like*.

You want to like the person you are about to speak with, so do what you would do for any potential friend, and get to know them! "Why spend the time?" you may ask. "Why not just ask them?" Doing your homework before you call shows initiative, takes your conversation to the next level, makes you feel more comfortable and, most important, shows that this job is important to you. Even if you don't get the job, this information will help you forge a new relationship that will be more gratifying and may even be helpful in your next interview or your new job.

Dealing with Rejection

We all have an invisible, imaginary scale in our brains, a measurement between "acceptance" and "rejection." When we're employed at a job we enjoy – with adequate income and reasonable benefits – that scale is tipped heavily toward the acceptance side. When we lose a job, the scale immediately tips toward rejection. Every subsequent failure – resumes not acknowledged, negative phone conversations, failed job interviews – keep adding to the weight on the rejection side of the scale. It is important, critically important, to counterbalance that rejection with the success of acceptance. Only then can we stop worrying about the consequences of every decision.

I know from extensive talks with unemployed professionals just what it is they want. It almost sounds childish, but it is quite simple and therefore basic. They want someone to make ALL of their decisions EVERY day, and at the same time make sure they will find a new job equal to or better than the one they've just lost. What a heavy burden would be lifted then! That way of thinking is a natural consequence of feeling rejected. Rejection saps your energy, robs you of the ability to think clearly, and crushes your self-esteem. It doesn't happen in one day, and there is not a single source, but you need to start by minimizing the rejections.

We've already seen how sending out hundreds of resumes increases the number of rejections, but there are other sources of rejection, too: blind Internet ads, job boards that don't provide contacts, and most employment agencies. You don't have to swing at every pitch: that's a good way to strike out. Reduce the number of rejections by selecting the pitches that you can hit. Would you really want to work for a company that treats potential employees like a meat market? That tells you something about the company right there – not to mention the fact that, since most of the resumes will be trashed AND 70% of jobs are obtained through personal referrals, your chance of getting that job is virtually nil.

To find job opportunities: (1) Use those four powerful words: "I need your help" finding job opportunities. Put the word out among your friends. You may find that you're one of a handful of candidates for a job that is never even advertised. (2) Look for jobs where you can build a bridge to the decision-maker. You only need one hit to change the game, so be more selective.

When you minimize rejection and focus on better quality opportunities, you have a better balance of victories, which include positive phone calls, job interviews and a deeper understanding of the people and companies with which you're interacting. In other words, your job search will be more meaningful.

Job Interviews: Selling Yourself

The unsuccessful phone call is one symptom. But even when it's successful and leads to an appointment, there is one more hurdle ahead: the job interview. Let's make sure that doesn't get off to a bad start. I'm always amazed at how many interviewees spend most of their precious time reiterating what is clearly on their resume. Think about that: if you didn't have the basic qualifications that the company wants, you wouldn't have been invited to an interview! They already know what you've done so far in life, from your formal education to most recent job experience.

Why simply repeat what they already know? **Give them new and important information about yourself**. Show that you've done your homework and impress them with what you know about the company and about the position you'll be filling. But that's getting a bit ahead of where we should be right now. There are several important things you should know and do before you walk through that interview door. You're dressed appropriately, and you've arrived at least 15 minutes before the scheduled appointment. So you're on track and on time.

Let's say you have a 3 p.m. appointment and you're sitting in the reception area of the office. What's going through your mind? Here's what some actual interviewees have told me: "Boy, I'm going to knock them dead! I'm going to convince them that I'm the person for this job! I'm really going to sell myself!" Sound familiar? These are stock answers, and, while not technically wrong, this is a way to "pump ourselves up," to prepare mentally for the stress that is part of any job interview. However, if I were to ask, "What do you think <u>the main objective</u> should be for this interview?" you might not be able to answer so easily.

Suppose I say that you should have only ONE objective? Separate yourself from the other candidates. <u>Ask how many others are being considered for this position</u>. Let's say they are going to interview seven. Once you know that, your objective is to be different from the other six. The person you're talking to is going to mull over the qualities and characteristics and personalities of all seven candidates. What's going to set <u>you</u> apart? What's going to make you stand out from the others?

Job Interviews: Some Tips that Make A Difference

You can be the one whose name, face, and conversation come to the interviewer's mind first, and stays there even when the rest are reviewed mentally in turn by knowing the most about the company, the industry, the job, the competitors, the interviewer, and what you have to offer. Knowledge is power, so prepare meticulously for your interview.

Most companies and organizations have web sites that describe what they do (or, more realistically, the image they would like to project), so that's a good place to start. However, dig a little deeper. If the company is public, you can learn about things like the company's cash flow and what analysts think of the company on brokerage sites like Etrade and Scottrade, or, if you don't have an online brokerage account, on sites like the Wall Street Journal, Google Finance or BigCharts.com. Find out what customers think of the company by searching for the company name, visiting Internet rating sites and searching for the company's name with the word, "sucks," after it. That may seem strange, but you'll often learn how customers really feel.

There's another reason to learn as much as you can before the interview: you may not want this job! If you're starting to feel negative during your preparation, you'll know the right questions to ask. Many unemployed professionals have told me that they "just want to get a job," Some have gone back into the workforce, and, within a few months, they're unhappy. It was the first job they were offered, and they took it.

Who are good sources of information about his company? Whom do you ask? Let's say this company makes widgets. Who buys them? Who are their rival widget makers? You have to <u>personalize</u> this job interview. You must have enough specific information in your mind to impress the interviewer with how much you know, and with exactly how you are going to help this company do a better job of designing, manufacturing, and marketing widgets. You have to **let them know HOW YOU FIT IN**.

What contacts do you have in the business world that can help the company? You may have great people skills, and you want to be a sales manager. You must demonstrate your ability to use those special techniques to increase sales. That's one way to set yourself apart, but the most essential way is this: while you're sitting in that waiting room, and when you enter the office or interview room, look around you. Observe what you see carefully – photos, paintings, furniture. These things will tell you something about the person in front of you.

Is he or she a camper? Sports enthusiast? Book lover? Family oriented? Direct some part of the conversation to that particular interest. If you share the same enthusiasm or interest or hobby, make sure it gets into the conversation. Don't be phony and pretend an interest in something that bores you. Find something personal that you can share, and make the interviewer aware that you know something about it or appreciate it in some way. Later, when that individual is going back over the list of interviewees, your interest in home repair or baseball or Hollywood films or rock music will suddenly resonate. "Oh, yes. This was the person with solid experience as a sales manager. But she is also crazy about soccer. Or stamp collecting. Or classical music." That's a shared interest, and it will count as a plus for you.

This is critically important. If you're the <u>only</u> one who mentioned something of personal interest that related to that person's background, or <u>you</u> got that person's positive attention for whatever reason, *then you have the edge on those who didn't*. We all make decisions based on what seem insignificant factors. Consider buying a house. Homebuyers may concentrate at first on the lawns, the garage space, and the heating or air conditioning units. They may also look critically at the bathrooms, kitchen, winter or summer sun exposure, proximity to their jobs or availability of schools for their children, but when they go home to weigh and balance everything, including overall cost, what may tip the scales on whether they buy that place (or the one they looked at last week) is the location and layout of the laundry room. *The smallest room of the house became its largest selling point.*

That's how decisions are made. Pay attention to all the little details when you're in a job interview, including how the interviewer dresses, and his or her body language. Observing these, interpreting them, and using them to your advantage can help to "level the playing field" at the very least, and it can ultimately make the difference in whether you or one of the other six get the nod. I know from years of talking with unemployed professionals that this is one of the most important factors in job-hunting. It is something that you must learn to trust implicitly. It's very subjective, but it's never wrong. It works, and it can work for you.

One More Tip – "Don't Do It Unless You Win!"

Let's look together at some other ways to win: for instance, phrases on the phone or your work ethic during the day. We've established that the resume, the phone interview, and the personal interview are the main sources of rejection. Let's try to make tomorrow better than today, next week better than this week, next month better than this month. We can do this by creating victories – tiny ones at first, and slowly. We want to get that "scale" or "balance" in our heads to begin weighing on the side of acceptance, not rejection.

The only way to feel acceptance is to experience "wins." Here's a way to remember this critical lesson that should be engraved on your brain, painted on your bathroom mirror, and displayed on the dashboard of your car:

DDIUYW

DDIUYW stands for "Don't Do It Unless You Win." If you're in favor of what the self-help books call a "Pro-Active Attitude to Life," then this is the slogan for you! If you can learn to make this a central part of your life for the next three to four months, this acronym will not only help you make decisions, but save you an enormous amount of grief. What most people don't give the unemployed – blue collar or white collar – much credit for is being extraordinarily perceptive. Those who are unemployed are very intuitive; they are able to sense something before it happens.

We've lost the right to earn a living, but we have this one compensation: like someone who has lost their eyesight, another sense has become more acute.

Losing a job, losing one's livelihood, is like that. It creates in the unemployed person the enhanced ability to "read" people perfectly. You can tell on the phone if someone's interested in you – how that person is responding to you, what questions you're being asked. That ability is enhanced in a one-on-one interview in someone's office: there you can tell as much by body language (facial expressions, gestures, etc.) as much as by tone of voice and language used just how you're doing.

By using that gift of acute perception and avoiding as best as possible the sting of rejection, life becomes easier. What do you say on the phone? What are some useful hints? What tone of voice should you use? Your objective is to get yourself into a personal interview. That's going to happen only if you stand out as <u>different.</u> **You want the person who will interview you to realize that you have something to offer the business, which the other candidates do not**.

Thus the more you can demonstrate knowledge of the position you're after, your knowledge of the company's history and policies and goals, the more you can score a victory on the telephone. **The more you know about the person who is interviewing you, and about the ultimate decision-maker for this position (if they are not the same person,) the more likely it is that you will score a victory**. You need every victory you can gain. Getting someone to respond to your resume is one. Getting someone on the phone to schedule you for an interview is another. "Nailing" that job interview – knowing that, when you leave it, you have either secured the job or are one of the top two or three candidates – is yet another.

Chapter 4

Creating Your Own String of Victories

Little Victories Add Up: Getting the "*Positive* No"

You can, using DDIUYW, manage little victories each day that will lead to the **big** victory you're seeking in a job equal to or better than what you had before unemployment. Even the sense of NOT doing something can be a kind of victory: NOT wasting time endlessly fine-tuning a resume, NOT spending useless time on the phone talking to the wrong person, NOT memorizing unimportant information that isn't going to enhance your personal interview. Let's go back to the phone: "Hi, I'd like to speak with Susan Jenkins." This can be a bit tricky. This will seem strange, but you want to get the person on the other end to say "No" in a way that will be helpful to you. This is what I call a "positive" NO.

Let's say you manage to get through to Ms. Jenkins just long enough for her to say "I'm sorry, I'm too busy to talk now." Here's your golden opportunity. Don't pass it up. Say to her, "I understand completely, Ms. Jenkins. I know you're busy. Let me ask you a question: You wouldn't have any objection if I got back to you in five or six days, would you?" She's going to say "No." No is easy to say.

People can say "no" without moving their lips. **But by saying "no," she's really given you permission to re-**

contact her. She knows you realize she's busy, and she knows you're not "pushy" in the sense of trying to get her to spend time on the phone with you <u>that minute</u>. You're willing to wait for a better time, and that makes <u>her</u> more willing to take your next call.

That's a victory. You've opened up the opportunity to make an appointment, through her assistant or secretary, with her approval. You've also made personal contact with her that she can recall. You've gained some insight regarding her telephone "manner," that is, her reaction to being called by someone she probably doesn't know. All of these are little victories, and you can build on them when you actually call the next time. By the third or fourth time you call, if it takes that many times, she'll be familiar with you. Even better, if you couldn't find a personal referral when you first called, you may have, by then, learned that someone you know actually knows <u>her</u>. That someone has had time to put in a good word on your behalf.

That's another victory. It may be the one that gets you the personal interview with Ms. Jenkins. By then you're an individual, a person, not just a name she doesn't recognize on the phone. You're already off to a good start. All of this comes down to you becoming "street smart" about unemployment. Maybe you didn't realize that you had to develop those "smarts." You do. You're in competition for a job, and there are more people looking for jobs than there are jobs. That's the simple mathematics of it. There are phrases and nuances that take time to learn. It takes trial and error.

I've said many times: in unemployment, a person goes from complete certainty to complete ignorance. As we noted above, that can happen in a matter of weeks, days or hours. All of a sudden, you're out of a job. A few months ago, life was great. You were a decision-maker in your own business, everything was "cool," you had the respect of your boss, of your colleagues, the admiration of your family and friends. You knew your routine; you had the assurance of a regular paycheck and reliable benefits. Now you're out of a job, and your life is suddenly filled with uncertainty. Every day is a puzzle and a problem. You're someplace you've never been before, you're enveloped by ignorance.

Please feel free to experiment. I'm trying to explain what your objections should be and to give you the tools to achieve them, but ingenuity is the key concept in this program. I like to think that everyone who buys this book has some imagination, and some innate ability to use their own skills and talents with the practical guidelines and advice offered here to find a better job. Use your newfound "street smarts" to adapt these ideas your own job search. You have to find the best way to get to that decision maker. When you're on the outside looking in, it's difficult to penetrate that "wall" into their environment, but it's not impossible.

Here's another victory you can achieve, but it takes real organization. It's called "setting your own appointment." Set an appointment to "work the phones" – let's say 10-11:30 a.m. on Tuesdays and Thursdays – and make your business contacts in the hope of getting a job interview. You'll have a list of perhaps 15 people you will call. You'll have their names and their phone numbers. You will have jotted down some notes about each position in each company. You're going to ask for a name, and review the method outlined above regarding how to **get that person to say "no" in a way that's a victory for you**.

Now you'll try to get phone interviews for the following Wednesday, let's say at 9 a.m. and another at 10:30. Maybe you can fit in two more that same afternoon. So the results of these Tuesday and Thursday initial contacts will be to have a full day of phone interviews scheduled for that next Wednesday. Think of how you'll feel when you wake up that day. You have a full schedule. Any one of them could lead to a job interview. **That's a victory**. By setting aside those three hours a week for making the phone appointments, you've moved forward.

You've also done it in such a way that you've avoided the pitfalls of going about it in a disorganized fashion. You don't want to start out by saying one day, in a bit of a panic, "I've got to start phoning." You get out some hasty notes, and you start in. You're not really prepared. You begin to feel the rejection at the other end, the feeling that you're making the wrong approach. By the time you've worked yourself into that list, you're losing your effectiveness. That's why you have to organize what you do and FOCUS. Don't spend more than an hour and a half per day on your phone calls. That way, you stay fresh, and stay alert.

You'll sound positive, and you'll get positive responses. Don't set yourself up for rejection because you're some place you've never been before. **Know whom you're asking for. Be short and sweet. Set up that "positive no."** Try to set up your appointments for the same day, so that you wake up with a full schedule ahead.

NEVER get on the phone out of guilt. Avoid it at all costs. That's setting yourself up for rejection <u>before</u> you get started, before anyone even has a chance to "blow you off" because you've come across to them as unprepared and disorganized. Victories on the phone come from (1) knowing who to ask for and (2) getting to the point, and (3) taking "no" for an answer – <u>a positive "no!"</u>

Creating a Victory – How One Person Did It

These are victories. Let me give you an example from reality, based on the case of an unemployed professional who went through the TLC program. Let's call her "Mary." Seminars were always followed a week or ten days later by a brief "How are things going?" workshop. I asked this young woman, a trained nurse, how she was doing. She was looking for work after being laid off by a hospital that was forced to downsize when budget restraints were announced.

She had found out who the decision maker is by asking a fellow worker in that hospital. Then she discovered something important about that person. It turned out that "Betty", the woman who might hire her, belonged to a hiking club. "Mary" enrolled in that same hiking club, and, on the very first hike, quite by chance, she was placed in the group of hikers with Betty. Obviously, Betty had no idea that Mary was one of the applicants for the job.

During the course of that hike the two women struck up a conversation, and Betty discovered that Mary was a trained, licensed nurse. That gave Mary the opportunity to say *"I've heard a lot of good things about your hospital. It must be a great place to work."* That's the correct procedure. Everyone loves a compliment. Those words are <u>magic</u>. They can open a conversation into areas that will work to your advantage.

In this case, Betty asked Mary about herself, and learned that she was at that moment looking for a job.

By the time they'd returned from the hike, it was clear that Mary had the right qualifications. They agreed on an appointment date and time, and Mary got an interview with someone who already knew her personally and had a clear idea of her capabilities. Mary got the job, in large part because she had used important personal knowledge to her advantage. **That was a major victory**.

Dealing with a Defeat – A Sample Scenario

While I'm on the subject of "victories," let me give you an example of what I consider to be a defeat. Remember the motto we noted above: **DDIUYW**? Here's a theoretical case where the person involved didn't keep it in mind. Suppose someone says to you: "Send a cover letter and a resume to Tom Brophy. He's the decision maker at XY&Z, Inc." You're very excited because you have a specific name of the person who will decide who gets hired.

So you prepare the letter and the resume. Here's what you shouldn't be saying in that cover letter: "Dear Tom Brophy, Please find enclosed a list of all the great things I've done in my life. PS: Please find something for me to do." Have you written anything that sets you apart? This is a blind resume. It expects the person who receives it to match your qualifications with some position that may be available at XY&Z, Inc. Do you think that this person is going to drop what he or she is doing to accommodate your vagueness? No. Your resume will go into the "circular file."

Keep in mind that YOU would have the same reaction that this decision-maker had. Let's put it another way in a simpler scenario. Let's imagine it's a snowy, cold Saturday morning in February. You're at home and the front doorbell rings. A guy is standing at the door and he says to you: "Hi. My name is William Murphy. I'm unemployed, but I'm handy with all kinds of house and yard work. I wonder if you have something for me to do."

You may, if you're feeling compassionate, be responsive in this way: "Let me take your phone number, Bill. If something comes up later in the spring, I'll give you a call." Does that sound familiar? It should, because it's the most common refrain of someone who's NOT going to call later in the spring, or ever. Now go back to that scenario. You're still home after "Bill" leaves. Nine other persons ring your bell and say approximately the same thing that Bill said. You've given the same answer to all ten. But the eleventh person says: *"How about if I shovel your driveway for $20?"*

He's made you an offer, and you have to respond. So you quickly think about how your day is shaping up and what you want to do. Shoveling your driveway isn't on the top of your list, so you're more likely to say: "Fine. Let me know when you've finished. I may want you to shovel the back sidewalk as well."

The point is that *you had to decide at once*, and, given the specific offer and the weather circumstances *at that moment,* you're more inclined to say "yes" than "no." **Remember: you've always got to make the offer specific, attractive and reasonable if you want to get attention**. The person reading your cover letter needs to see that you know EXACTLY what position is being advertised, and the attached resume shows why your qualifications and experience EXACTLY match those specific job requirements.

Organizing Your Time

Victories come in all shape and sizes. How do you spend your day? How do you organize your time? What are you finding out about the decision-maker for each and every job advertisement to which you're responding? Organize every week. Mondays might be good for research (getting the background on specific business or institutions or agencies). Tuesdays and Thursdays are telephone days – limited to just 90 minutes in the morning, 90 minutes in the afternoon.

Give yourself a break. This is a marathon, not a sprint. Set up an exercise program. Pick a day and go out to lunch with a friend. Learn how to get selfish and "re-charge your batteries." *The biggest victory that an unemployed professional can experience is a returned phone call or email.* Imagine that just three months ago a returned phone call might mean very little – it was something you expected within the routine of your job. Now it becomes the difference between a victory and a defeat. You're the judge. You're the jury. If you organize your time, you'll experience the crucial difference between the two. Remember: **DDIUYW**.

How important are victories? Even little ones? Victories to the unemployed professional are like water to a person in the desert. Go a week without water and you're physically dead. Go 12 to 15 weeks of job hunting without a victory and you're spiritually dead. It's that critical. From my experience over many years, I know the lights go on when people recognize that they *need* victories and that the same tired approach to job-hunting is hollowing them out.

Imagine that a dear friend had come to you a year ago. He or she is unemployed and feeling depressed. No doubt you're compassionate enough to sit down and talk it through. I'm sure your friend would feel better. We can do that for others, but it's next to impossible to do for ourselves: we can't make ourselves feel better through internal conversations. We need to change the behavior that is hurting us.

Once we've lost a job, part of our difficulty in functioning is that we feel we don't <u>belong</u>. It's not as easy as it sounds to remove ourselves from the situation, to draw back and to be objective. We set ourselves up for rejection and don't see ourselves doing that. *Don't touch the stove when it's hot!* It's going to hurt. But we constantly touch it, rejection sets in, and slowly we slip away into depression and despair.

When I conduct unemployment seminars, I tell the participants: "This is probably the only group of people you're going to be with, the only situation you'll be in, where you won't have to finish the sentence. Everybody in the room can finish it for you. And, of course, you can do the same for someone else in this room." I give some examples: I may say to someone at random: "Steve, why aren't you with your last employer?" Inevitably there is hesitation.

I then ask everyone else in the room: "Did you get anything from that question?" Just as inevitably the hands go up and the answer comes back: *"Yes. Steve's searching for an answer."* Whenever we're confronted with such a question regarding unemployment, we always search for the right words. Because the memory is painful, and putting painful or shameful experiences into words is not easy. It helps to know that everyone else in that seminar room feels the same way.

One last piece of valuable ammunition you should have available at a second's notice is an "elevator speech," a 20-second verbal blurb you can give while riding in an elevator. It covers who you are, what you are about and what you bring to the table. You need to have it ready at all times. Practice it…. Memorize it.

Unemployed professionals are a family of extremely bright and sensitive people. They have special gifts. Once you realize the pitfalls of job searching, it won't take you long to catch on. Even the most intelligent of us can be gullible when we're in a situation for the first time. We're not where we belong.

Becoming Selfish: Caring for Your Inner Person

Let's imagine that you're recently married, and you have your first child, Amanda. As new parents of a six-month-old, you're obviously concerned with Amanda's every sniffle and cough. Let's also imagine that the main wage earner becomes unemployed. You take Amanda to the pediatrician for that first major check-up, and the doctor says, "Amanda has an inner-ear problem that is going to affect her equilibrium as she gets older. It's a rare condition, but it's correctable. There are perhaps three doctors in the country who can perform this type of operation."

That's all the information you would need. Is there any doubt in your mind that you'd find the best doctor? Of course not. It is a classic example of "We can't do it for ourselves but we **can** do it for others." You see, deep inside each one of us there is a "little person," someone we can usually ignore or at least take for granted. But that "little self" is vulnerable and, in the present circumstances, can feel great pain and distress. Take care of that "inner self." Nurture that person. Become selfish. Use whatever it takes to get to the decision maker who can, like the specialist with Amanda's inner ear ailment, rectify a problem that is disturbing your equilibrium. You need to work hard to improve your own mental health. You need to maintain a healthy lifestyle, which includes exercise, good eating, spiritual re-enforcement and a handpicked support group around you. This support group could consist of golfing friends, church friends or anyone who can give you honest feedback.

"I've Got A Secret" Hardly A Game Show

I hope this struck a few responsive chords to make you aware that you're not alone – and that your pain is not a chronic ailment that somehow goes undiagnosed and can never be treated. Unemployment is a very emotional condition, but there's a brighter side to it.

You may remember a TV reality show called *The Fear Factor*. Contestants were brought face-to-face with a situation, an object, or a demand like having to eat insects or worms, which forced them to confront their own fears or disgust. Sudden and unexpected unemployment is another type of "fear factor" in our lives. In a flash, it's there in front of us and we have to deal with it.

We all have secrets when we're unemployed, and the only persons who might possibly understand and share those secrets are other unemployed professionals. You will "take that secret to the grave" with you, or so it seems. Here's a common secret: let's say you've been unemployed three months. You're out shopping for food in the local supermarket on a Tuesday at 10 a.m. Suddenly, you imagine that people you pass in the aisle are aware of your situation. You get the distinct and uncomfortable impression that their eyes are on YOU. Then the conversation within you starts: "These people must know something's wrong in my life. Why else would I be here shopping on a workday morning? They must know I lost my job. How can I pretend I don't notice the stares, and how can I get out of here without meeting some person I know who will start asking questions?"

Everyone who's reading this knows that feeling. We're out of work long enough for it to make a big difference in our daily routines. Whenever we are around a group of people, we think we are wearing some special sign across our chests that proclaims: "I'M UNEMPLOYED. I'M DIFFERENT FROM YOU. I'M BROKEN!" It's not really there but it seems so. Every morning of your unemployment, you have the same conversation with yourself when you awake. "Today I'm the Lone Ranger. No one is going to help me." You reconfirm that each day, and you never tell a soul about it…….. Not your spouse…… Not your children……. Not your best friends. And certainly not strangers you meet in the canned vegetable aisle of the local Whole Foods or Costco.

Inner Dialogue – Hiding the BIG Secret

We all talk to ourselves when we're unemployed. Would you like to know what the NUMBER ONE secret of unemployed professionals is? I'll share it here, because it's something you probably wouldn't share. The persons closest to the unemployed professional all give the same impression, and they all reach the same mistaken conclusion. THEY ALL THINK YOU KNOW WHAT YOU'RE DOING! Guess what? YOU DON'T KNOW. YOU DON'T HAVE A CLUE. Not only that. YOU CAN'T TELL THEM THE TRUTH. So you continue to hear the same phrases that bring more comfort to them than to you.

You know them by heart. "How's he doing? He's fine. He's sending out resumes. He's making phone calls for job interviews. He is just days away from a new job. Everything is OK. He's on top of the situation!" The reality is quite different. You are not OK. You're not on top of anything – except maybe a pile of unpaid bills! Yet you can't say anything to anyone. In my seminars, as soon as I make that observation, the normal and immediate reaction is: "How did you know that about me?" How do I know? Here's how: "Been there, done that!" Remember my personal tale of how I lost a business during one visit by one person who informed me that the shop I rented was no longer available, and I'd have to move? That's all it takes: one brief announcement and your life is turned upside down and inside out.

I've felt that. The problems and anguish are not endemic to the East Coast of the U.S. or more severe to one group of people than to another. These conditions and feelings are just as prevalent on the West Coast, in the South and in the Midwest. We're also wise enough not to be "comforted" by the periodic announcements from federal or state governments that "unemployment is down." That may mean that some unemployed have simply stopped looking for jobs: they are no longer a "labor statistic." They're still unemployed, but they no longer register on a radar screen.

No one ever talks about the emotional side of unemployment. It's much easier to talk about "resumes" and "phone calls" and "appointment schedules," but, as every marketer knows, emotions are what drive us.

I can't sell myself if I don't feel good about myself. Let me tell you something: you are a winner; you're one of a kind. You're not a statistic, not to me and not to anyone else who truly knows you. There is no one else on earth like you. You are precious, so take care of yourself and try to help others who are seeking employment. You're going to use this time wisely, and you're going to use it well. I can say that with confidence because I know what others like you have told me, and I've been there myself. This is NOT a dead-end situation. Someone is listening to you, and someone cares about you. You just need to find the right people and deliver the right message.

Chapter 5

On the Outside Looking In

A Light At the End of the Tunnel

Unemployment is an emotional dilemma. It causes daily frustrations that you alone must bear, and that others, no matter how sympathetic, cannot affect until the problem is solved and you find another job.

When you observe someone who has been unemployed for months, you can see that frustration up close and personal. As a loved one, you want to be compassionate and caring, to show understanding. You'll say: "I know it's tough. I know what it's like. I know what you're feeling." The first few times, that little speech may actually help the person to know that you care, but when he or she has heard it for the twentieth time, it's become another reminder that there is still no light at the end of the unemployment tunnel.

Now matter how sincere a spouse or a friend might be, they cannot truly feel the other person's pain. When we're unemployed, whether our spouse or children want to admit it or not, our family status (at least in our own hearts) has been reduced. We second-guess ourselves when we discipline our children, and think we can see the look in their eyes: "Dad/Mom, you're out of work. It's not the same any more. You're no longer the person of authority you used to be," and, "How can you tell me to work harder when you don't even have a job?"

That is a killer. Nothing can destroy one's self-esteem faster than to see that message in the eyes of a child. I've talked to many people who are experiencing long-term unemployment and one of the things they find most difficult to talk about is precisely the fact that they no longer feel like a provider for their family. Even in a situation where both spouses work, when one is unemployed the balance shifts and the out-of-work partner feels inadequate.

A lot of these feelings have to do with the chemistry of family life; when a well-established pattern is altered, there are often serious consequences. Even without the threat of losing the house or losing medical benefits, the unemployed spouse can't help but feel carried along by the one who works. It is a change that children sense immediately, and it is painful.

These are all symptoms of unemployment that are not just difficult to deal with, but are almost impossible to talk about. Yet keeping them inside just feeds the growing sense of frustration, so it becomes a vicious cycle, repetitive and corrosive and then, with no solution in sight, debilitating. You take these feelings to bed, and they are there when you wake up. That's one of the hardest realities of being an unemployed professional.

We need to create situations that create victories; otherwise we're spinning our wheels. We need to get the emphasis away from what you're doing wrong, and the daily rejections and defeats which they are providing, and get on the right track: remember that motto? "Don't Do It Unless You Win!" If you don't read my resume, if you don't return my phone call, I'm still on the outside looking in. You need to erase that feeling of not belonging. That is rejection, plain and simple. In time, we become sensitized to it just as we become sensitive to certain pollens or spores or chemicals. We become allergic, and we start avoiding the cause of the allergy. Or we start to medicate ourselves in an effort to reduce the discomfort of the allergic reaction.

Think of it in terms of a person going out repeatedly to take a sun bath in a field that's full of poison ivy. We wouldn't knowingly do that a second time if we had an immediate and severe allergic reaction. But let's say we come back with only a mild itch, and we're told it might be just from grass stains, so we repeat the process, and the next time the symptoms are a bit worse. Finally, we wake up to the fact that we're doing something wrong, repeatedly, and we need to avoid it completely. That's what happens when we experience those little rejections in job hunting that, when allowed to continue unchecked, produce the huge feeling of frustration, pain, and social dislocation. Like the sufferer from a bad case of poison ivy, we begin to isolate ourselves from family, friends, neighbors, and associates. We begin to feel we've set ourselves up for defeat, and yet all along we've been following the rules.

"Y.A." and Me – How I Met a Giant

At some point in our lives, we've all experienced some form of "preferential treatment" that made us feel important. I want to tell you how it made me feel to meet a legendary athlete when I was a young man.

I was 19 years old, in college, and a big fan of the NY Giants football team. A group of us decided we would drive to Cleveland to watch the Giants play the Browns. It happened to be Thanksgiving weekend, and, before we left on our weekend road trip, I came home to spend

Thanksgiving with my family in Princeton. Thanksgiving morning, a friend of my father called to invite me to his home to meet someone special.

When I arrived, I was introduced to Y.A. "Yat" Tittle, the star quarterback of the Giants, and one of the greatest passers of all time. Tittle's 36 touchdowns in 1963 were the most touchdown passes ever in a single season. That same year, Tittle passed for seven touchdowns in a single game, a record that still stands.

Yat invited me to toss a football with him in a public park in Princeton that morning. "Yat" throwing ME a pass! Can you imagine what a thrill that was to a 19-year-old? I worked up enough nerve to tell him I'd be in Cleveland that weekend, and hoped he could arrange for me to visit the Giants dressing room and meet the others on the team. Tittle said: "No problem. Just show up at the dressing room door when the game is over. I'll have a priest bring you in. Just pose as my nephew."

My buddies and I drove out to Cleveland, sat through that freezing game, and, shortly before it was over, I made my way to the dressing room. The place was jammed with sports reporters. I thought, "No priest is going to show up to escort me through this mob." Just then a priest appeared. I slowly inched my way toward the priest through the large crowd. I tugged on his sleeve and asked politely "Can I see my uncle?" He asked, "Who is your uncle?" "Y.A. Tittle," I said. He said. "Tom, you come with me." He headed toward the dressing room door and that crowd of reporters parted for us just like the Red Sea did for Moses and the Israelites! I was on my way to meet the Giants!

Yat was just inside the door. "Hi, Broph," he said. "Come on in. I want you to meet our captain, Joe Walton." I was on Cloud 9. An unforgettable moment, to say the least. THAT is a victory! That is an example of preferential treatment. We have all experienced it at least once and some of us more often. At that moment, I could not have felt more special.

Suppose your next-door neighbor sold tickets to a big event happening near you. Wouldn't you try to get your neighbor to sell you front row tickets at a discounted price? That's "networking:" finding someone who can help you. That is great way to achieve a great victory.

There is nothing wrong with being treated preferentially. We sometimes feel like we don't deserve special treatment, but let me ask you this: do you deserve to be treated poorly? Do you deserve to be out of a job? Of course not. You are unique, you have skills, and you deserve to be ushered into some inner sanctum where you are appreciated. Your friends can help you find that place.

Everything revolves around victories, small at first, and then progressively larger. Did you ever notice that there is a direct relationship between "being out of the loop" or "being broke" or "being tired?" Did you ever notice that wealthy people seem to have an abundance of energy? Successful people are accustomed to preferential treatment. In fact, they demand it. Instead of frustration, they feel empowered to dream more, ask for more, and do more. You can, too.

"Momentum" – Turning Defeats into Victories

When you are unemployed for several months, you begin to feel that debilitating fatigue that comes with repeated rejection. You don't want to pick up the phone again because you don't want to be rebuffed again. Your energy is drained, and your self-esteem has hit rock bottom.

To borrow another sports analogy, you need to turn the game around, to change the momentum. In any sport, there is a moment when spectators sense that the direction of a game has changed. Sometimes the shift is subtle as it can be in baseball: what appears to be a final "out" turns out to be a critical "walk"; there's a runner on base and the next batter gets a hit. The pitcher hits the next batter. Suddenly, the bases are loaded; the team on the brink of extinction has the winning run at the plate. The next pitch gets hit into the upper deck and the entire game is turned around.

Something like this happened in 2004 for the Boston Red Sox in the American League playoff against the New York Yankees. The Yankees had dominated the league for so long that Yankees fans would shout, "1918!" to remind the Sox of the last time that they had won the World Series. By October 17, 2004, the Yankees had swept the first three games of the AL playoffs. Ahead by one run in the eighth inning of the fourth game, the Yankees brought in Mariano Rivera to pitch.

Mariano Rivera is widely considered the best "closer" in the history of baseball. In postseason play, Rivera has the most saves, the lowest earned run average, the most consecutive scoreless innings, and has saved almost 90% of every game he has entered. Rivera shut down the Red Sox in the eighth inning with a strike and two ground outs.

The Red Sox were three outs away from losing another series to the Yankees when they came to bat at the beginning of the ninth inning. Then the momentum changed: Kevin Millar drew a walk (a little victory.) Next, Dave Roberts, pinch-running for Millar, stole second (another little victory.) Then Bill Mueller hit a single to tie the game (a bigger victory!) Rivera retired the side on a sacrifice bunt, a strike out and a pop-up. The Red Sox had not won, but they had changed the momentum.

The game was scoreless until the bottom of the 12th inning when Red Sox left fielder Manny Ramirez singled, and designated hitter David Ortiz hit a walk-off home run to win the fourth game 6 to 4. Even so, the Yankees still needed to win just one more game to win the series, but the Red Sox won the next three straight games to become the first team ever to come back from a three game deficit – not to mention being one inning away from losing the fourth game! The Red Sox went on to win their first World Series in 86 years by beating the St. Louis Cardinal in four straight games!

For the Red Sox, two little victories led to bigger and bigger victories.

I'm sorry to repeat this painful story for Yankees and Cardinals fans, but it demonstrates how momentum can change, and how, no matter how far down you are against spectacular odds, when the momentum turns, you can go from the edge of the pit to the peak of the mountain.

Be constantly on the alert for that one instance when an opportunity presents itself and you can turn the momentum in your favor. You can't predict that moment, but, when it comes – if you're ready for it – it will result in that one victory that leads to many others. No matter how insignificant that victory may seem, that is the "win" you need to get back on track. That change of momentum can propel you to the next bigger victory, and you will sense the change.

Here's some even better news: unlike the Red Sox and the Yankees, you decide how many innings you want to play. Unless you're sick or you quit, you're still in the game. History is full of great people who were defeated or despised, but who stayed in the game until the momentum changed.

In order to get to tomorrow, though, something good has to happen today. If enough defeats and rejections pile up today, you may feel like tomorrow will NEVER come or that you wish it would NOT come! Failure is just as contagious as success, so it's important to be attuned to momentum, both negative and positive. When you minimize rejections and maximize victories – even small ones – you'll turn the momentum in your favor.

Marriage is very similar. Why are some marriages successful, and others not? Durable marriages make both spouses feel important. We get lots of small victories from each other. Frequent rejections are toxic, and they can lead to the dissolution of the marriage. You can turn around a marriage, too, by developing strategies to minimize rejections and maximize small, daily victories.

Getting Results – Some Rules for the Road

Once we understand that if we continue taking "the wrong road" back to the world of work we will probably never get there, we've already achieved something important. Learning to read the "road signs" correctly is essential, and that is why I spent so much time above pointing out the pitfalls (resumes, phone contacts, personal interviews) that can beset the unwary. I know from experience that some of us approach job hunting in a scattershot manner: "If I throw enough stuff (resumes, phone calls) against the wall, some of it will stick (one resume or phone call will bring a positive response.)" Sure, sometimes that WILL work, but it usually doesn't.

We all know the drill. You've been to college, earned a useful degree, gotten a job with a company that looked "solid," worked your way up the corporate ladder to some position that generated a comfortable salary and benefits and provided a satisfactory intellectual challenge and then, BAM! You learn that the entire unit where you work will be eliminated because of technological developments or financial downsizing or outsourcing or whatever. So you're OUT. You put on the "happy face," talk to friends, collect benefit checks, begin to grind out those resumes and expect that unemployment is going to be just a few weeks of "paid vacation."

Then you begin to realize it "just ain't so." The statistics support your conclusion. The average unemployed professional who had earned a salary of $60,000 per year is out of work 13.5 months, which is more than a year of hell – or, more accurately, three months of "coma" when you're still trying to make sense of it all followed by ten months of hell when you realize how much skilled, experienced competition there is for the few available jobs in your particular field. That's when you suddenly experience the shock of being out of work for more than a year, and you're thinking that there is no end in sight.

The first step to victory is when you realize that what you're doing is NOT working. Perhaps that's why you're reading this book. You realize that you've been misinterpreting the road signs, that you're spinning your wheels while others zip by with clarity and purpose. You feel like you have no clout, that you have a secret to hide and that you're an outsider.

Fortunately, you now understand the symptoms of unemployment and you can see that you have a lot in common with everyone who has ever been unemployed. You may be on the outside looking in, but you also have a new sense of how things work. You know who's real and who's phony; trust that sense. You know that the hiring system is deeply flawed, and, most important, I hope that you are starting to think about why you deserve a break – why you DESERVE preferential treatment and how you're going to work to get preferential treatment from your network of friends and associates.

It's time to start focusing carefully and consistently on gaining that one small victory, that one "win" amid all the losing that will demonstrate that there is a way out – that the momentum has turned in your direction. The "rules of the road" are there to read: minimize rejections; maximize your victories. Re-gain your confidence. DDIUYW. Make tomorrow better than today.

Chapter 6

Stability, Strategy, and Success

"I Haven't Got a Clue"

Recently, I received a call from an unemployed professional who had just lost his job. Let's call him "Joe." Joe's annual salary had been in the range of $100,000. Since unemployment paid $600 per week, he was dependent on bi-weekly unemployment benefits checks of $1,200 each, which would usually cease after six months because benefits last only 26 weeks (though they have been extended during the current recession.) In a short conversation, I could tell that Joe was still in shock. To some basic questions about his severance package, Joe replied, "I haven't got a clue." This man, who enjoyed broad authority within his former position, now had no idea what to do next.

In my experience with unemployed professionals, many used the phrase "I don't know" hundreds of times in the first three months. What they don't know could fill a small book, which, in a sense, is in your hands now. They make the wrong decisions – sometimes expensive decisions – because they're not familiar with the new neighborhood. They get caught up in that unemployment traffic jam, and, before they know it, they've set themselves up for rejection. One defeat turns into many, and, soon enough, they are either stalled on the shoulder of the road to another job.

Odd Person Out Syndrome

It's like a bad dream – especially when that impersonal "they" turns into the very personal "you." You find yourself somewhere you've never been before, and you don't know what to do first. You start keeping secrets, and the biggest of them is: "I need someone to make ALL my decisions." Not just to tell you who to contact and what forms to fill out for unemployment benefits, but how much cream and sugar to put in your morning coffee. Every daily decision that never caused any concern before is now magnified to such a degree that it weighs on you. You want someone to lift that heavy load and, ultimately, to find you that job.

You feel helpless, and others begin to sense that maybe you are beyond help. If you don't "belong" where you are, your chances of succeeding or making friends or of finding another job are severely diminished. To use another baseball analogy, it's like trying to get invited to a "pickup" game with kids from another neighborhood. Remember the routine? Two captains take turns choosing teams from the available players by working their hands hand-over-hand to the top of a bat. The last hand on the bat gets to pick first. Unless everyone knows that you're the best player on the field, you watch silently as other kids are selected, leaving you the odd one out. If you've never played sandlot baseball, the rough equivalent of that humiliation is sitting in a middle school or high school dance and watching everyone else being asked to dance.

It's humiliating, and the experience leaves a scar. If those kinds of scenes are repeated, the sense of rejection only deepens. Now, transpose that to the world of unemployment. Looking for a job in a competitive market is like trying to be noticed so that you'll get picked for the sandlot softball team or the school dance. That is why even a small, seemingly insignificant victory is important, and why a positive ratio of victory to rejection is important. Build your confidence. Stop sending resumes to blind advertisements. Don't Do It Unless You Win! And don't let your bottled-up frustrations betray you later....

Stay Cool, and Keep Your Anger Out of Interviews

Never let anger and frustration get in the way of your success. Most of us are angry about being down-sized, fired, or let go. No matter how it was explained, someone decided that we were no longer needed, and most unemployed professionals happily sabotage themselves by telling the truth about their previous work experience. This is a natural inclination that stems from good ethics and the chance to vent, but it is not helpful to you.

Inevitably, your prospective employer asks, "Why aren't you with your last employer?" It's been eating away at you over the weeks or months, and you want to respond, "Because the S.O.B. never appreciated what I did for the company" or "We had a big earnings loss two quarters in a row, and I was the handiest person on which to pin the blame." I'm sure you can think of a dozen others. Once you've expressed your resentment, though, you've provided your interviewer with information that he or she has no right to know.

Think twice before you answer such a question. You are in competition with many others for that same position. Be circumspect. <u>Don't divulge anything about yourself that is less than positive and upbeat</u>. Don't give away your secrets, even if they are painful, and your recollection of them is honest and accurate. Look at it like this. When you enjoyed a "date" with someone who caught your fancy, you didn't divulge every detail about yourself. In particular, you didn't share every nuance of when, why and how your last relationship ended – especially if you were "dumped." The person with whom you may have a lasting relationship can learn all about that in due time.

When a question comes your way that might evoke a negative, angry, or resentful response, especially about the details of your present status, think like someone who is learning karate – divert the pain. Go on with the interview. When another probing, potentially damaging question comes your way, block it. Don't get sidetracked. Divert and block. Don't get aggressive. "Why aren't you with your last employer?" You respond. "I got caught in a downsizing." That's a common, acceptable answer. Memorize it. Practice it. Don't hesitate when you hear the question. Your future employment may depend on it. Keep it short, keep it neutral, keep it impersonal, and keep it in the past.

Customize Your Strategy – One Size DOESN'T Fit All

When I went to college, I used to take a bus from Princeton to Niagara Falls that required a layover in the New York Port Authority Bus Terminal. While I waited in New York, I would observe the hundreds of passengers who walked by. The one thing that distinguished each and every one of them was their manner of walking. It is distinct for every human, and as unique as a fingerprint. I was mesmerized by the number of personal walking styles.

I think of those walking styles when I think about how you may take my advice. Every reader will interpret my recommendations to fit your own manner of personal interaction. You will customize these strategies, which is really the best possible solution. If hard and fixed rules led to new jobs every time, the whole process would be smooth and predictable, but that would ignore your individual style, your dreams, and the fact that the job market constantly changes. My goal is to offer principles to help you avoid the roadblocks and traffic jams along the way, and to point you in the direction of greater victories and fewer rejections.

Those who regain employment the quickest are often those who are the most creative in their job hunting. When people tell me about their resumes, phone calls, and the whole "paper trail" along the road to re-employment, they often complain, "How come I'm not getting anywhere?" The answer is in the repetition: if it hasn't worked the first 50 times, it's unlikely to work the next 50 times. If your process isn't working, stop and re-think your approach. Isn't it time to innovate?

A man named Graham Healy used to demonstrate on TV that anyone can do certain household chores quickly and easily, utilizing ordinary, inexpensive ingredients and some common sense that eliminates the repetitive, expensive and labor-intensive methods of those same chores. He just showed alternative ways to approach household tasks, and convinced you that it is worth your while to try it.

I can remember as a kid being asked to help my mother clean all the sterling silver flatware and tableware – everything from forks to candlesticks. She would give me some pink gunk on a cloth that I had to scrub into the silver, and then it all had to be washed and dried carefully so that there were no water stains. It took lots of scrubbing. The oxidized black stain got all over my fingers, and the chemical compound in the cleaning paste smelled terrible. That was the traditional way to clean silver, and I never questioned it until I discovered Graham Healy. He takes some water softener, vinegar, baking soda and a gallon or so of lukewarm tap water, and then mixes that concoction in a plastic tub.

Then comes the magic. Into the tub, Healy puts a piece of aluminum foil. Then he takes a silver candlestick with some fancy filigrees and ornamentation that are especially hard to clean, and dips it into this absolutely simple, common, non-toxic solution; then he removes the candlestick and lets it dry. Bingo! That candlestick is cleaner than any chemical scrubbing could ever get it, and it took no more effort than to mix the ingredients. THAT is innovation! Better results with less work. So after you've sent out your 150th resume and made your 50th phone call, consider my methods for getting through to the decision maker, avoiding rejection, and coming up with a plan that will make you happy.

Don't forget that out-of-work nurse who learned from a friend that a prospective employer (and "decision maker") liked to hike. Her genius was following through on the tip and then meeting that person in such a way that it seemed serendipitous. Pain and disappointment do NOT have to be part of the unemployment process. You are intelligent enough, perceptive enough, and creative enough to think of ways to reach the person who will make the critical decision about who will be hired for the position for which you are qualified. Use the techniques in this book to become the top choice on that decision maker's list.

Why I love what I do

Over the past twenty years I've worked with hundreds of unemployed professionals to avoid the customary pitfalls into which the unwary usually fall. Some people say that I'm "street smart" about unemployment. It's not just that "I've been there, done that" in my own working life, but I've learned these methods from people who have successfully and, more quickly than others, re-entered the workforce.

I've worked with "strangers in a strange land" and helped them find ways to get back to familiar territory. It's been my pleasure to provide encouragement and a gentle push in the right direction. Once you know that your feelings of embarrassment, rejection, frustration, fear, and social isolation are all symptoms of the unemployment, you can begin to heal the mind by treating the symptoms, just as you would heal the body by treating a fever.

If you're unemployed, you have a new, heightened intuition that can help revise your thinking. You are closer to reality than you have been in years, and you don't have to believe that the employment world works the way that it's advertised. It doesn't. Believing in that system of resume-and-rejection can only hurt you.

Graham Healy showed me how faulty that thinking can be. He demonstrated clearly and credibly that there is no "one way" to do anything, whether it's cleaning the family silverware or searching for a job. For unemployed professionals, rejection is the greatest barrier to getting yourself back on track. Instead, build your little victories into that Big Victory of a rewarding job commensurate with your skills and experience. There is no substitute for victories, and you cannot compromise until you've felt the special pleasure of ending every day by celebrating more victories than rejections.

This fundamental realization came from speaking with over 40,000 unemployed people over the last dozen years. I've learned the language of unemployment, which, like every profession, has its own jargon that is initially incomprehensible. It's all part of the culture shock – that initial "coma" into which we slip when the reality of unemployment dawns on us.

Many companies provide unemployment advice after the exit interview in thick, esoteric binders. Accepting these weighty tomes, you are supposed to feel as if you've received something valuable and useful, but you've mainly received a heavy black binder. As anthropologist Margaret Mead was fond of saying: "If you can't explain something basic and important to a ten-year-old child, then you probably don't understand it yourself." Such binders were created by people who were never unemployed, and haven't recently helped anyone find a job. They are guilt offerings wrapped neatly in plastic.

The trauma of unemployment creates its own learning disability. Try talking with someone who has just endured a serious car accident without major physical injury. On the surface, they may appear fine, but they are probably suffering emotionally and mentally. They may suffer amnesia, nightmares, or pain that arrives after the initial surge of adrenalin is gone. At the very least, they are disoriented and unable to make simple decisions. They need a temporary car; they need help from their insurance company; they need clear, concrete, specific assistance. They DON'T need complex charts and diagrams, or detailed and distracting "strategy sessions."

Logjams and roadblocks stand between a world of self-doubt and a world of self-worth, between the day that you were "let go" and the day that you accept a new job offer. The good news is: now you know the neighborhood.

You know new routes to take. You can start building upon little victories today in preparation for bigger victories tomorrow.

One more story…

I once visited the National Frontiers Trail Museum in Independence, Missouri, which is where many of the western frontier trails began. The museum features the stories of settlers and their extraordinary struggles. One story – the story of John Bidwell – has stuck with me.

In 1839, 19-year-old John Bidwell secured a claim of 160 acres in Platte County, Missouri, where he hoped to build a life for himself. This was a substantial piece of property! Bidwell must have been excited about his prospects, his chance to establish his own farm and perhaps his plans for a family. He left his property for four weeks to earn money and buy supplies, but, upon returning, Bidwell found that his claim had been "jumped" and that, since he was neither 21 nor the head of a family, he could not establish legal title to the land. Bidwell lost everything – his job, his property, and his hope for a future in Missouri. Imagine how disappointed he must have been.

About that time, Bidwell heard about California, and joined one of the first parties to journey over land to that distant territory. It was a dangerous and virtually uncharted trip, but here is what happened to John Bidwell after he lost everything:

Bidwell met John Sutter, discovered gold, was made a general in the army, established the city of Chico and became one of the wealthiest people in California. He was elected to the U.S. House of Representatives, and ran for Governor of California and President of the United States.

In 1864, he was a member of the committee that notified Abraham Lincoln of Lincoln's second nomination. President Andrew Johnson and future president Ulysses S. Grant attended Bidwell's wedding. John Muir, Leland Stanford, William T. Sherman, Susan B. Anthony, and other prominent people of his day visited his home.

Losing 160 acres in Missouri is hardly a footnote in the life of John Bidwell. While it must have been crushing at the time, it was probably the best thing that ever happened to him.

I sincerely hope that the loss of your job will lead, like John Bidwell's loss, to an improvement in your life. I hope that you get a better job – perhaps the kind of job that you have always wanted. I hope that reading this book will help change your momentum, and that you'll start building *Little Victories* that lead to bigger ones. I hope that this incident will be but a footnote on your way to the happiness you have always imagined.

Appendix 1

Don't Do It Unless You Win!

Maximize your wins; minimize your rejections. Print this (or tear it out of the book), and cut-and-paste where needed: bathroom mirror, dashboard, tattoo parlor, wherever you can remind yourself to focus on your wins.

DDIUYW

DDIUYW

DDIUYW

DDIUYW

Appendix 2

Summary of Phone Techniques

The phone is your friend, and it is the best way to make friends. People tend to hire people they like, and you can make a personal connection with a phone.

Your goal is to make an APPOINTMENT for an interview.

Imagine you are an entertainer and you're preparing for a concert next week. How much time do you spend rehearsing your performance? 3 hours, 4 hours, 2 days, 3 days? Whatever the time, it is certain you WILL be prepared to be the best you can be.

Treat every phone call like a concert performance.

1. Get to the decision maker: know the name of the person you want to reach.

2. Get a referral: 70% of jobs are obtained through referrals.

3. Use LinkedIn, Facebook and other networking opportunities to work through a chain of people beginning with your own contacts until you can find a referral to the person who is hiring.

4. When setting up your referrals, use these powerful words with your friends: "I need your help!"

5. Be confident and practice your pitch and your voice mail.

6. If it takes time to do this, so be it.

7. Make your call short, sweet, and to the point.

8. Know exactly what you're going to say.

9. Allocate 1.5 hours for 12 to 14 calls every day.

10. "Google" anyone you intend to call. If it's worth making the call, it's worth knowing something about that person.

The Call

Hi, Mr./Ms._____. I'm_____.
Our mutual friend _____ asked me to give you a call. I have something I want to talk over with you. When can we get together?

The Positive "No"

You wouldn't mind if I called you back next week, would you?

Appendix 3

Little Victories List

Our lives are a series of little victories that bring us happiness and lead to bigger victories. Here are some daily, little victories to seek or celebrate.

- Trusting your ability to read people

- Exercising in the morning and getting energized for the rest of the day

- Researching companies and opportunities in your area

- Finding out the name of the decision maker

- Eating a healthy meal

- Preparing an organized phone session (1.5 hours max)

- Making a phone call because you want to; NOT getting on the phone out of guilt

- Getting to the decision maker with whom you can establish a personal connection

- Getting a phone call returned

- NOT sending a resume out to a blind advertisement or someone whom you don't know

- Setting up a voice message that is upbeat and positive

- Maintaining social contact; celebrating your friends with an email, phone call or lunch

- Having a good conversation or a laugh with your spouse

- Making three valid business contacts in a day

- Learning some new skill for your profession

- Taking a little vacation every day – one to two hours to read, hike or do something that you enjoy

- Praising your children

- Getting a "positive no"

- Saving money

- Praying for others in the same situation

- Being open – sharing your situation with a friend

- Volunteering for a charity where you can help someone face to face

- Getting a good night's sleep

- NOT doing something because it conflicts with **DDIUYW** – Don't Do It Unless You Win.

- Knowing that you've done your best

- Learning a new idea

- Sending Tom Brophy an email to comment or ask a question… tom@tbrophy.com

- Customizing the principles in this book for your own style!

Made in the USA
Charleston, SC
21 July 2010